THE
PRACTICAL ORGANIST
50 Short Works for Church Services

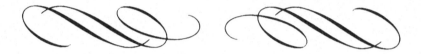

Alexandre Guilmant

Selected and Edited by
Samuel P. Warren

DOVER PUBLICATIONS, INC.
Mineola, New York

Bibliographical Note

This Dover edition, first published in 2001, is a reordered but otherwise complete and unabridged republication of works in *The Practical Organist: A Collection of Organ Compositions with Pedal Obbligato by Alexandre Guilmant / Edited by S. P. Warren,* originally published in two volumes by G. Schirmer, Inc., New York, 1889. A prefatory note, list of contents, and alphabetical title index are newly added.

We are grateful to The Sibley Music Library, Eastman School of Music, for making these rare volumes available for republication, and to organ scholar Rollin Smith for his kind advice during the preparation of this reorganized edition.

International Standard Book Number

ISBN-13: 978-0-486-41686-1
ISBN-10: 0-486-41686-0

Manufactured in the United States by LSC Communications
4500053882
www.doverpublications.com

PUBLISHER'S NOTE

Between 1871 and 1880, Alexandre Guilmant privately published and sold his organ pieces for church services, issuing his Opp. 39, 41, 46, 47, 49, 50, 52, and 55–59 in twelve installments *(livraisons)* under the group title *L'Organiste pratique.*

In 1889, G. Schirmer, Inc., New York, issued fifty pieces from that work in a two-volume set published as *The Practical Organist: A Collection of Organ Compositions with Pedal Obbligato by Alexandre Guilmant.* The music, then reengraved, was selected and prepared by Schirmer's renowned editor Samuel P. Warren, with English titles and registrations replacing the original French.

While retaining the idea of twelve installments (now called "books")–but for reasons left unexplained in his edition–Warren reordered Guilmant's original plan, resequencing the music in an entirely new menu of the editor's own design. Guilmant's original *5e livraison,* for example, was devoted to the six pieces of Op. 49; Warren's "Book 5" consisted of four pieces in this order: Op. 47/2, 49/5, 55/5, and 47/3.

The present publication reprints Warren's exemplary edition in a single volume, restores Guilmant's original sequence of pieces, and corrects a handful of inaccurate opus numbers.

CONTENTS

ALPHABETICAL TITLE INDEX

THE PRACTICAL ORGANIST

50 Short Works for Church Services

Elevation
in F major.

Op. 39. № 1.

Offertory

in **A** major.

Registration:
- Swell: 8 & 4' to Oboe.
- Choir: 8 & 4' Foundation Stops.
- Great: Diapasons with Ch. coupled.
- Pedal: 16 & 8' — Gt. Coupler.

Op. 39. № 2.

Allegretto. (♩ = 100.)

Manuals.

Pedal.

(Gt. Uncoupled.)

Gt. to Ped.

6

March
in D major.

Registration:
Swell: Diapasons 8 & 4′ with 8′ Reeds.
Great: *p* = 16 & 8′ *ff* = Full. (Sw. to Gt.)
Pedal: *p* = Bourdons 16 & 8′ *ff* = Full, with Gt. Coupler.

Op. 39. № 3.

Manuals.

Pedal.

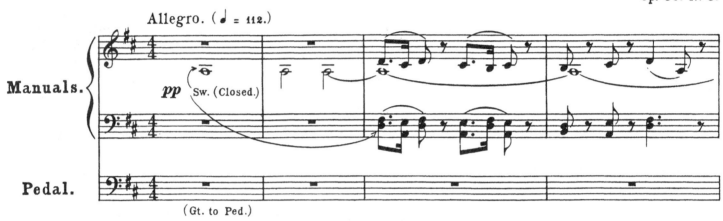

12

Two Anthems.

No. 1. For a 2d Tone. (10th tone transposed.)

Andante. (♩ = 66.)

Op. 39. No. 4.

Manuals.

Pedal.

Nº 2.

Andante con moto. (♩ = 84.)

Manuals.

Pedal.

Communion
in E minor.

Adagio. (♩ = 56.)

Op. 39. No 5.

Manuals.

p Sw. Voix celestes & Gamba.

Pedal.

p

Bourdon 16′ Sw. to Ped.

cresc.

dim.

Offertory
in C minor.
ON CHRISTMAS CAROLS.

Registration:
Swell: Oboe & Stop. Diap. 8´
Great: Full.
Choir: Harmonic Flute 8´
Pedal: Full with Gt. Coupler.

Op 39, Nº 6.

Andante grazioso. (♩=72.)

Variation.

Sw. (Ob. in, draw Vox humana with Tremulant.)

(Tremulant in.)

Prelude

in E♭ major.

Registration: { Great, Choir & Swell coupled: 16, 8 & 4´ Found. Stops
{ Pedal: 32, 16 & 8´ Found. Stops. Gt. Coupler.

Op. 41, No 1.

Andante sostenuto. (♩ = 69.)

rit.   a tempo.

Magnificat

in G major.

FIRST VERSE IN PLAIN-SONG.

Op. 41, No 2.

Registration:
Swell: Stop. Diap. Flute & Vox humana with Tremulant.
Great: Soft 8′
Pedal: Soft 16 & 8′

Registration:
Swell: Oboe only. Stop Diap. ad lib.
Choir: Harmonic Flute 8
Pedal: Soft 16 & 8

Duo Pastorale.

Un poco Allegretto e grazioso. (♩=138.)

Manuals.

Fugato.

Allegro moderato. ($\bullet$=126.)

34

Funeral March

in C minor.

Registration:
Swell: Horn (or Oboe) & Stop. Diap. 8′
Great: Stop. Diap. 16 & 8′ Harm. Fl. 8′
Choir: Quintaton (or Stop. Diap.) 16′ Harm. Fl. 8′
Pedal: Soft 16 & 8′

Op. 41, N⁰ 3.

Andante maestoso. (♩ = 66.)

Gt. to Ped.

37

(Sw. Voix celestes in,
draw Horn (or Oboe.)

Cantabile
in F major.

Registration:
{
Swell: Stop. Diap. Harmonic Flute 8′ & Oboe.
Great: Stop. Diap. & Clarabella (or Harmonic Flute) 8′ with Sw. coupled.
Pedal: Soft 16 & 8′ Stops.
}

Andante. (♩ = 76.)

Il canto ben legato.

Op. 41, № 4.

Processional March

in A major.

Op. 41, No 5.

D. C. senza replica.

Elevation

in E minor.

Op. 41, № 6.

Communion
in D major.

Registration:
Swell: Stop. Diap. Gamba & Harmonic Fl. 8 & 4′
Great: Stop. Diap. Salicional & Clarabella (Sw. Coupler.)
Pedal: Stop. Diap. (Bourdon) 16′ & Bass. Flute 8′

Andante. (♩ = 80.)

Op. 46. N⁰ 1.

Legato.

Manuals.

Pedal.

Strophe.

For the Hymn "ISTE CONFESSOR."

(2nd Mode transposed a tone higher.)

Op. 46, № 3.

Postlude

in F major.

52

Melody
in **G major.**

Registration: {
Swell: Harmonic Flute & Clarionet (or Oboe) 8′
Choir: Dulciana or Stop. Diap. 8′
Pedal: Stop. Diap.(Bourdons) 16 & 8′
}

Molto Adagio. (♩ = 46.)

Op. 46. № 4.

Manuals.

Pedal.

March
in F major.

Op. 46. Nº 5.

Registration:
Swell: 8 & 4′ Fluework with 8′ Reeds.
Great: Full. with Couplers.
Choir: 8 & 4′
Pedal: Full with Reeds.

Allegro maestoso. (♩ = 58.)

Fine.

60

D. S. senza replica sin' al fine. Gt. **ff**

Offertory

in E♭ major.

Registration: { Swell: Diapasons.
Great: Diapasons, with Sw. coupled.
Pedal: 16 & 8′.

Op.46, N⁰ 6.

Allegretto non troppo.(♩ = 69.)

Manuals.

Pedal.

64

Canzona

in F minor.

Registration:
Swell: 8 & 4′ Flutes.
Great: Salicional, & Stop. Diap. 8′.
Choir: Bassoon, Clarinet & Stop. Diap. 8′.
Pedal: Soft 16 & 8′.

Op. 47, No 1.

Un poco più mosso.

Grand Triumphal Chorus

in A major.

Registration:
- Solo: Reeds.
- Swell: All the 8 & 4 Ft. Stops.
- Great: Full with Sw. Coupled.
- Pedal: *ff* Full. *p* =16 & 8 Ft.

Op. 47, Nº 2.

Allegro maestoso e marziale. (♩ = 63.)

Manuals.

ff Solo.

Gt.

Pedal.

ff

Gt. to Ped.

ten.

Solo.

Gt.

ten.

ten.

ten.

p Sw.

p legato.

Off Gt. Coupler.

Gt. to Ped. add Reeds. ff

Off Gt. Coupler.

p

Gt. to Ped. add Reeds.

78

*) These detached chords are obtained by coupling and uncoupling the SOLO to GREAT by means of a pedal coupler. (Where the coupling is effected by a draw stop, an assistant will be necessary.)

80

Bomb. 32 Gt.

Offertory
in C minor.

Registration.
Swell: Harmonic Flute & Viol. di Gamba 8′
Choir: Soft 8 & 4′
Great: Open Diap. Stop. & Clarabella 8′ Sw. Coupler.
Pedal: Soft 16 & 8′ Stops.

Op. 47, № 3.

Allegro moderato. ($\quad$ = 100.)

Manuals.

Pedal.

Gt. to Ped.

83

84

Prayer
in B♭ major.

Registration: { Swell: Stop. Diap. & Viol di Gamba 8′ (or Voix célestes.)
{ Pedal: Stop. Diap. (Bourdons) 16 & 8′

Op. 47. № 4.

Adagio. (♩ = 56.)

Manuals.

Pedal.

Absolution.

E minor.

Registration:
Swell: Vox humana & Stop. Diap. 8′ with Trem.
Choir: Dulciana & Harmonic Flute 8′.
Great: Salicional & Stop. Diap. 8′. Ch. coupled to Gt.
Pedal: Bourdons 16 & 8′.

Op. 49, № 1.

Offertory
on "O filii."

Registration:
{
Swell: Full.
Choir: 8 & 4'
Great: = *ff* = Full. *p* = 16 & 8'. with Sw. & Ch. coupled.
Pedal: = *ff* = Full *p* = 16 & 8'. (Gt. Coupler.)
}

Op. 49, № 2.

Allegretto. (♩ = 66.)

(Reeds in.)

dim.
Ch.
(Prepare Sw. Vox humana & Stop.)
Diap. 8' with Tremulant.

O Filii.
Andante. ($\bullet = 96$.)

pp
Sw.

(Gamba & Stop: Diap. 8' only.)

(Sw. Uncoupled.)

96

Allegretto

in B major.

Registration:
- Swell: Stop. Diap. Flute Traverso & Viol. di Gamba 8′
- Choir: Echo Dulciana 8′ (or Salicional.)
- Great: Stop. Diap. Clarabella & Gamba 8′ with Sw. coupled.
- Pedal: Sub bass 16′ & Bass Fl. 8′

Op. 49, Nº 3.

100

Fuga "alla Handel"

in F major.

Op. 49, № 4.

Choral
in **G** major.

Registration: { Swell: Diapasons 8 & 4'
{ Great: Diapasons.
{ Pedal: 16 & 8'

Op. 49, Nº 5.

Adagio. (♩ = 58.)

Manuals.

p Gt.

Pedal.

p Gt. to Ped.

Four Versets.

Op. 49, N? 6.

110

Invocation
in E♭ major.

Registration:
Swell: Voix Celestes, Gamba & Stop. Diap. 8′.
Great: Salicional & Stop. Diap. 8′.
Pedal: Soft 16 & 8′.

Op. 50, N<u>o</u> 1.

The Manger.

(LA CRÈCHE.)

PASTORALE AND ADORATION.

Registration:
- Swell: Stop. Diap. Gamba, Harmonic Fl. 8 & 4'
- Great: Stop. Diap. & Harmonic Flute 8' with Sw. coupled.
- Choir: Vox Angelica.
- Pedal: Soft. 16 & 8'

Op. 50, № 2.

117

120

Postlude

FOR THE FEAST

of the Assumption of the Holy Virgin,

ON THE HYMN: INDUANT JUSTITIAM.

Op. 50, N.º 3.

124

In - du - ant ju - sti - ti - am,   Præ - di -

Plain song.

dim.

cant læ - ti - ti - am,   Qui mi - ni - stant nu - mi - ni.

Grand Chorus

IN MARCH FORM, IN GREGORIAN TONALITY.

Op. 52, N⁰ 1.

128

Madrigal

in E♭ major.

Registration:
{
Swell: Stop. Diap. 8′ & Vox humana with Tremulant.
Great: with Ch. coupled: Stop. Diap. Clarabella & Salicional 8′.
Choir: Har. Fl. 8′ or Stop. Diap. Dulciana, Soft 4′ Fl.
Pedal: Sub. Bass or Bourdon, 16′ & Bass Fl. 8′.
}

Op. 52, N.º 2.

(Open Diap. in.)
Ch..

Gt.

Ch.

(Gt. & Ch. Uncoupled.)

Andante con moto

in F major.

Registration: { Swell: Soft 8 & 4'. Great: Soft 8' Sw to Gt. Pedal: Soft 16 & 8'.

Op. 52, No. 4.

Allegro non troppo
in A minor.

Registration:
Swell: (Closed) Diapasons 8′
Great: Open Diap. Stop. Diap. Harmonic Flutes 8 & 4′ Sw. to Gt.
Pedal: Soft 16 & 8′

Op. 55, Nº 1.

142

Scherzo Symphonique
in C major.

Op. 55, № 2.

Registration:
Swell: All the 8, 4 & 2′ Stops. Reeds.
Great: *f* = 16, 8 & 4′ Trumpet, Clarion. *p* = 16, 8 & 4′ with Sw. coupled.
Pedal: 16, 8 & 4′

Trio I.

Gt. Coupler in.

cresc.

(Sw. open.)

f Trumpet, Clarion.

non legato.

Sw.

Trio II.

Coda.

Più Allegro.

Bombarde 32.

Elegy

in F minor.

Registration:
Swell: Flauto traverso, Stop. Diap. & Viol di Gamba 8′
Great: Stop. Diap. Salicional, Clarabella 8′. with Sw. & Ch. coupled.
Choir: Quintaton (or Twelfth 2⅔′) Soft 4′ Flute.
Pedal: Soft 16 & 8′

Op. 55, No 3.

Strophes.

FOR THE ASCENSION HYMN.

Registration:
{ Swell: Stop. Diap. 8′ & Cornopean.
{ Great: Diapasons 8′.
{ Pedal: Soft 16′ & 8′.

Fourth Tone transposed a 4th higher.

Op. 55, № 4.

FUGATO.

Manuals.

Pedal.

Ite Missa Est.

Op. 55, N.º 5.

March

in **D** major.

Op. 56, № 2.

TRIO.

Allegro moderato e pastorale

in E major.

Registration:
- Swell: Diap. 8′ & 4′ with 8′ Reeds.
- Great: Diapasons 8′ with Ch. Coupled.
- Choir: Soft 8′.
- Pedal: 16′ & 8′.

Op. 57, № 1.

Meditation

in B minor.

Registration:
{ Swell: Voix celestes & Gamba.
{ Great: Soft 8'.
{ Pedal: Soft 16' & 8'.

Op. 57, N⁰ 4.

Andante quasi Adagio. (♩= 50)

Manuals.

Gt. *sempre legato.*

Pedal.

Prelude and Fugue

in E minor.

Registration: {
Swell: 8 & 4'.
Great: Diapason, with Sw. coupled.
Pedal: 16 & 8'.
}

Preludio.

Allegro. (♩ = 116.)

Op. 58, № 1.

181

Tempo I.

Cornopean in.

(Close the Sw.)

Andante con moto

in E♭ major.

Registration:
Swell: (Closed) Diapason 8′
Great: Open Diap. Stop. Diap. Salicional & Clarabella 8′ Harm. Fl. 4′ (Sw. to Gt.)
Pedal: Soft 16 & 8′

Op. 58, N⁰ 4.

add Sw. Cornopean.

Gt. to Ped.

cresc. - - - -

Torchlight March

(Marche aux Flambeaux.)

Registration.
- Solo: Reeds. (ad lib.)
- Swell: Full.
- Great: p = 16, 8 & 4 Ft. ff = Full. (Sw. coupled.)
- Pedal: p = 16 & 8 Ft. ff = Full. with Gt. coupler.

A Tempo moderato e molto maestoso. ($\downarrow$ = 72.)

Op. 59, Nº 1.

MANUAL.

PEDAL.

TRIO I.

TRIO II.

Sw. (Full.)

(16 & 8 Ft. Sw. to Ped.)

Communion

ON "ECCE PANIS ANGELORUM."

Registration:
Swell: Voix célestes & Gamba 8′.
Great: Soft 8′.
Choir: Clarion. & St. Diap 8′.
Pedal: Soft 16 & 8′.

Andante. (♩ = 120.)

Op. 59, № 3.

Bridal Chorus.

Registration:
Swell: 8 & 4′ Flutework & Reeds.
Great: *p* = 16, 8 & 4′ *ff* = Full with Sw. & Ch. coupled.
Choir: 8 & 4′
Pedal: *p* = 16 & 8′ *ff* = Reeds.

Allegro moderato e maestoso. (♩ = 100.)

Manuals.

Pedal.

legato.

Gt. to Ped.

214

Interlude
in E♭ major.

O Salutaris Hostia.

ELEVATION.

Registration:
- Swell: Vox humana, Stop. Diap. 8′ with Trem.
- Great: Harmonic Flute 8′ Sw. coupler.
- Pedal: Soft 16 & 8′.

Prayer
in **A flat**.

Registration:
- Swell: Vox humana & Stop. Diap. 8′ with Tremulant.
- Great: Stop. Diap. & Gamba 8′ with Ch. coupled.
- Choir: Salicional or Dulciana 8′
- Pedal: Sub bass or Bourdon 16′ & Flute 8′

Un poco Adagio. ($\bullet$ = 66.)

Offertory

in D major.

Registration: {
Swell: Stop. Diap. Gamba, Harmonic Flutes 8 & 4´.
Great: Diapasons.
Choir: Stop. Diap. 8´ Cremona or Clarionet.
Pedal: Soft 16 & 8´.
}

Andante con moto. ($\flat$ = 76.)

(Gt. to Ped.)

Sw. (open.)

p dimin. - - - - pp rall.

off Gt. Coupler.